Photographer • Jarek Duk
Art Direction & Stylist • Georgina Brant
Hair & Make Up • Zoe Kramer
Design Layout • Lindsay Birch for Quail Studio
Model • BMA Model Management

First published in Great Britain in 2018 by
Quail Publishing Limited
The Incuba, 1 Brewers Hill Road, Bedfordshire,
England, LU6 1AA
E-mail: info@quailstudio.co.uk

ISBN: 978-0-9935908-5-6

CLASSIC ESSENTIAL KNITS

eight hand knit designs

quail studio

Contents

Introduction

Classic Essential Knits is a collection of 8 designs from cardigans to sweaters.

The collection features timeless designs with a classic look. All styled in everyday wearable fashion pieces, the designs cover Rowan's core yarns and our signature Quail Studio style.

Whether it is the large wraparound shawl that can be paired with your favourite wardrobe staples, or the longline cabled cardigan, we have designed the collection to be easy to wear and stylish at the same time.

We have focused our design attention in this collection to really focus on the fit and shape of our knitwear designs, ensuring that after you have hand knitted your piece, it is comfortable and gives you the look that you were hoping for.

Taking inspiration from high street fashion trends, and pairing designs with a simple and refined colour palette, *Classic Essential Knits* is a collection that bridges the gap between our oversized designs and our more fitted fashion pieces.

q u a i l   s t u d i o

Gallery

Alice *pg 28*

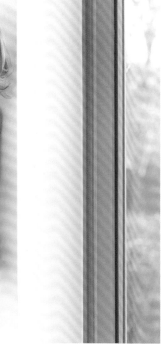

Annie *pg 30*

Betty *pg 32*

Ella *pg 36*

Grace pg 40

Ida pg 42

Mable pg 44

Marie pg 46

Alice

Rowan Kidsilk Haze
& Rowan Fine Lace pg 28

Annie

Rowan Kid Classic pg 30

Betty

Rowan Alpaca Soft DK pg 32

Ella
Rowan Kid Classic pg 36

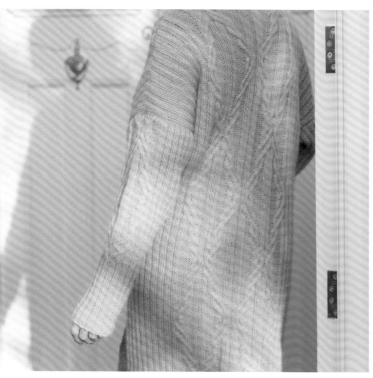

Grace

Rowan Cocoon pg 40

Ida
Rowan Brushed Fleece pg 42

Mable

Rowan Pure Wool Worsted
& Rowan Kidsilk Haze pg 44

Marie
Rowan Kid Classic pg 46

The patterns

Alice

SIZE

60cm/23½in wide and 220cm/86½in long

YARN

Rowan Kidsilk Haze and Rowan Fine Lace

1 x 25g ball of Rowan Kidsilk Haze
(photographed in shade Steel 664)
1 x 50g ball of Rowan Fine Lace
(photographed in shade Pigeon 950)

NEEDLES

6mm (no 4) (US 10) needles

TENSION

17 stitches and 22 rows to 10cm/4in measured over stocking
stitch using 6mm (US 10) needles and 2 strands of Rowan
Kidsilk Haze yarn and 1 strand of Rowan Fine Lace yarn
held together.

WRAP

Using 6mm (US 10) needles and 2 strands of Rowan Kidsilk
Haze yarn and 1 strand of Rowan Fine Lace yarn held
together throughout, cast on 102 sts.
Work in g st for 6cm/2¼in, ending with a WS row.

Next row (RS): K to end.
Next row (WS): K6, P to last 6 sts, K6.
Rep last 2 rows until work meas 214cm/84¼in,
ending with a WS row.

Work in g st for 6cm/2¼in, ending with a WS row.
Cast off.

MAKING UP

Press as described on the information page.

Annie

SIZES

To fit bust

71-76	81-86	91-97	102-107	112-117	122-127	cm
28-30	32-34	36-38	40-42	44-46	48-50	in

Actual size

89.5	103	110.5	119	131.5	140	cm
35¼	40½	43½	46¾	51¾	55	in

YARN

Rowan Kid Classic

6	6	6	7	7	8	× 50g

(photographed in shade Cement 890) – Yarn A

I	I	I	I	I	I	× 50g

(photographed in shade Smoke 831) – Yarn B

NEEDLES

5mm (no 6) (US 8) needles
5.5mm (no 5) (US 9) needles

TENSION

19 stitches and 25 rows to 10cm/4in measured over stocking stitch using 5.5mm (US 9) needles.

EXTRAS

Stitch holders

Stripe sequence
Yarn B = 2 rows
Yarn A = 4 rows

BACK AND FRONT (both alike)

Using 5mm (US 8) needles and yarn A, cast on 86(94,106,114,126,134) sts.
Next row (RS): *K2, P2, rep from * to last 2 sts, K2.
Next row (WS): P2, *K2, P2, rep from * to end.
Rep last 2 rows four more times, dec 1(0,1,0,1,1) st at each end of last row. 84[94,104,114,124,132] sts.

Change to 5.5mm (US 9) needles.
Starting with a K row, working in st st and stripe sequence, cont until back meas 38.5(38.5,41.5,41.5,45,45cm /15¼(15¼,16¼,16¼,17¾,17¾)in, ending with a WS row and on second row of yarn B stripe.

Break off yarn B and continue in yarn A only.

Shape armholes

Cont in st st, cast off 4(4,5,5,6,6) sts at beg of next 2 rows. 76[86,94,104,112,120] sts.
Next row (RS): K2, Sl 1, K1, psso, K to last 4 sts, K2tog, K2. 74[84,92,102,110,118] sts.
Next row (WS): Purl.
Rep last 2 rows to 70(80,88,98,106,114) sts.
Cont straight in st st until armhole meas 12(12,13,14,15,16)cm /4¾(4¾,5,5½,6,6¼)in, ending with a WS row.

Shape shoulders and back neck

Next row (RS): K23(28,32,37,40,44), turn, leaving rem sts on stitch holder.
Next row (WS): Purl.
Next row: Knit.

Next row: Purl.
Next row: K to last 4 sts, K2tog, K2. 22[27,31,36,39,43] sts.
Rep last 4 rows to 20(24,28,32,36,40) sts.
Cont straight in st st until armhole meas 20(20,21,22,23,24)cm /7¾(7¾,8¼,8¾,9,9½)in, ending with a WS row.

Cont in st st, cast off 10(12,14,16,18,20) sts at beg of next row. 10[12,14,16,18,20] sts.
Next row: Purl.
Cast off.

With RS facing, slip centre 24(24,24,24,26,26) sts onto a second stitch holder, rejoin yarn to rem sts and K to end.

Work as for other side of neck, reversing shapings.

SLEEVES (make two)
Using 5mm (US 8) needles and yarn A, cast on 38(38,42,42,46,46) sts.
Next row (RS): *K2, P2, rep from * to last 2 sts, K2.
Next row (WS): P2, *K2, P2, rep from * to end.
Rep last 2 rows four more times.

Change to 5.5mm (US 9) needles.
Starting with a K row, working in st st and stripe sequence, cont as follows:
Next row (RS): K2, M1, K to last 2 sts, M1, K2.
40[40,44,44,48,48] sts.
Working inc as set above, cont in st st, inc 1 st at each end of every foll 4th(6th,6th,4th,4th,4th) row to 76(76,80,84,88,92) sts.
Cont in st st until sleeve meas 49(50,51,52,53,54)cm /19¼(19¾,20,20½,20¾,21¼)in, ending with a WS row and second row of yarn B stripe.

Break off yarn B and cont in yarn A only.

Shape armhole
Cont in st st, cast off 4(4,5,5,6,6) sts at beg of next 2 rows. 68[68,70,74,76,80] sts.
Next row (RS): K2, Sl 1, K1, psso, K to last 4 sts, K2tog, K2.
66[66,68,72,74,78] sts.
Next row (WS): Purl.
Rep last 2 rows 4(4,5,5,5,6) more times. 58[58,58,62,64,66] sts.

Next row (RS): K2, Sl 1, K1, psso, K to last 4 sts, K2tog, K2.
56[56,56,60,62,64] sts.
Next row (WS): P2, Sl 1 purlwise, P1, psso, P to last 4 sts, P2tog, P2. 54[54,54,58,60,62] sts.
Rep last 2 rows to 2(2,2,2,4,6) sts.
Cast off.

MAKING UP
Press as described on the information page.
Join right shoulder seam using mattress stitch.

NECKBAND
With RS facing, using yarn A and 5mm (US 8) needles, pick up and knit 18 sts down left side of front neck, knit 24(24,24,24,26,26) sts
from front neck stitch holder increasing 1 st on last st, pick up and knit 18 sts up right front neck, pick up and knit 18 sts down right back neck, knit 24(24,24,24,26,26) sts from back neck stitch holder kfb on last st, pick up and knit 18 sts up left back neck. 122[122,122,122,126,126] sts.
Next row (WS): P2, *K2, P2, rep from * to end.
Next row (RS): *K2, P2, rep from * to last 2 sts, K2.
Rep last 2 rows twice more.
Cast off in rib.

Join left shoulder and neckband seam.
Sew in sleeves.
Join side and sleeve seams.

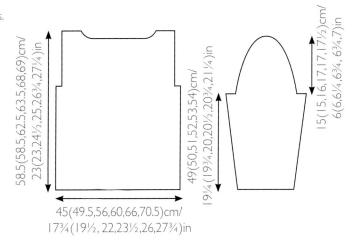

58.5(58.5,62.5,63.5,68,69)cm/ 23(23,24½,25,26¾,27¼)in

45(49.5,56,60,66,70.5)cm/ 17¾(19½, 22,23½,26,27¾)in

49(50,51,52,53,54)cm/ 19¼(19¾,20,20½,20¾,21¼)in

15(15,16,17,17,17½)cm/ 6(6,6¼,6¾, 6¾,7)in

Betty

SIZES

To fit bust

71-76	81-86	91-97	102-107	112-117	122-127	cm
28-30	32-34	36-38	40-42	44-46	48-50	in

Actual size

78	87	98	109	118	129	cm
30¾	34¼	38½	43	46½	50¾	in

YARN

Rowan Alpaca Soft DK

14	15	15	16	16	17	x 50g

(photographed in shade Charcoal 211)

NEEDLES

3.25mm (no 10) (US 3) needles
4mm (no 8) (US 6) needles
4mm (no 8) (US 6) circular needles at least 80cm/32in long

TENSION

22 stitches and 30 rows to 10cm/4in measured over stocking stitch using 4mm (US 6) needles

EXTRAS

Stitch holders
Stitch markers

BACK

Using 3.25mm (US 3) needles, cast on 106(114,124,134,146,158) sts.
Row 1 (RS): *K1, P1 rep from * to end.
Row 2 (WS): *P1, K1 rep from * to end.
Last 2 rows set moss st.
Rep last 2 rows twice more.

Change to 4mm (US 6) needles.
Starting with a K row, work 2 rows in st st.
Next row (RS): K2, Sl 1, K1, psso, K to last 4 sts, K2tog, K2.
104 [112,122,132,144,156] sts.
Working dec as set above, cont in st st, dec 1 st at each end of every foll 14th(16th,18th,20th,18th,18th) row to 86 (96,108,120,130,142) sts.
Cont straight in st st until back meas 51(51.5,52,52,53,53)cm /20(20¼,20½,20½,20¾,20¾)in, ending with a WS row.

Place a stitch marker at each end of last row to denote start of armholes.

Shape armholes

Next row (RS): K2, Sl 1, K1, psso, K to last 4 sts, K2tog, K2.
84 [94,106,118,128,140] sts.
Next row (WS): Purl.
Next row: Knit.
Next row: Purl.
Rep last 4 rows to 78(88,100,112,122,134) sts.
Cont straight in st st until armhole meas 21(22.5,24,25.5,27,29)cm /8¼(8¾,9½,10,10¾,11½)in, ending with a WS row.

Shape shoulders and back neck

Next row (RS): K26(31,36,42,46,52), turn.
Next row (WS): P2, P2tog, P to end. 25[30,35,41,45,51] sts.
Next row: Cast off 15(20,25,31,35,41) sts, K to end. 10 sts.

Cast off.

With RS facing, slip centre 26(26,28,28,30,30) sts onto a
second stitch holder, rejoin yarn to rem sts and K to end.
Work as for other side of neck, reversing shapings.

LEFT FRONT

Using 3.25mm (US 3) needles, cast on 124(133,142,153,164,176) sts.
Row 1 (RS): P0(1,0,1,0,0) *K1, P1 rep from * to end.
Row 2 (WS): *P1, K1 rep from * last 0(0,1,0,1,0)st,
P0(0,1,0,1,0).
Last 2 rows set moss st.
Rep last 2 rows twice more.

Change to 4mm (US 6) needles.
Starting with a K row, work 2 rows in st st.
Next row (RS): K2, Sl 1, K1, psso, K to end.
123[132,141,152,163,175] sts.
Working dec as set above, cont in st st, dec 1 st at side edge
of every foll 14th(16th,18th,20th,18th,18th) row to
114 (124,134,146,156,168) sts.
Cont straight in st st until work meas 51(51.5,52,52,53,53)cm
/20(20¼,20½,20½,20¾,20¾)in, ending with a WS row.

Place a stitch marker at beg of last row to denote start
of armhole.

Shape armhole
Next row (RS): K2, Sl 1, K1, psso, K to end.
113[123,133,145,155,167] sts.
Next row (WS): Purl.
Next row: Knit.
Next row: Purl.
Rep last 4 rows to 106(116,126,138,148,160) sts.
Cont straight in st st until armhole meas
21(22.5,24,25.5,27,29)cm /8¼(8¾,9½,10,10¾,11½)in, ending
with a RS row.
Break off yarn.

Shape shoulder and front neck
Next row (WS): Slip next 81(86,91,97,103,109) sts onto a
stitch holder, rejoin yarn and P to end. 25[30,35,41,45,51] sts.
Next row (RS): Knit.

Next row: Cast off 15(20,25,31,35,41) sts, P to end. 10 sts.
Cast off.

RIGHT FRONT

Using 3.25mm (US 3) needles, cast on 124(133,142,153,164,176) sts.
Row 1 (RS): P0(1,0,1,0,0) *K1, P1 rep from * to end.
Row 2 (WS): *P1, K1 rep from * last 0(0,1,0,1,0)st,
P0(0,1,0,1,0).
Last 2 rows set moss st.
Rep last 2 rows twice more.

Change to 4mm (US 6) needles.
Starting with a K row, work 2 rows in st st.
Next row (RS): K to last 4 sts, K2tog, K2. 123
[132,141,152,163,175] sts.
Working dec as set above, cont in st st, dec 1 st at side edge
of every foll 14th(16th,18th,20th,18th,18th) row to
114 (124,134,146,156,168) sts.
Cont straight in st st until work meas 51(51.5,52,52,53,53)cm
/20(20¼,20½,20½,20¾,20¾)in, ending with a WS row.

Place a stitch marker at end of last row to denote start
of armhole.

Shape armhole
Next row (RS): K to last 4 sts, K2tog, K2.
113 [123,133,145,155,167] sts.
Next row (WS): Purl.
Next row: Knit.
Next row: Purl.
Rep last 4 rows to 106(116,126,138,148,160) sts.
Cont straight in st st until armhole meas
21(22.5,24,25.5,27,29)cm /8¼(8¾,9½,10,10¾,11½)in, ending
with a WS row.
Break off yarn.

Shape shoulder and front neck
Next row (RS): Slip next 81(86,91,97,103,109) sts onto a
stitch holder, rejoin yarn and K to end. 25[30,35,41,45,51] sts.
Next row (WS): Purl.
Next row: Cast off 15(20,25,31,35,41) sts, K to end. 10 sts.
Cast off.

SLEEVES (make two)

Using 3.25mm (US 3) needles, cast on 58(60,62,62,64,64) sts.

Row 1 (RS): *K1, P1 rep from * to end.

Row 2 (WS): *P1, K1 rep from * to end.

Last 2 rows set moss st.

Rep last 2 rows twice more.

Change to 4mm (US 6) needles.

Next row: K2, M1, K to last 2 sts, M1, K2. 60[62,64,64,66,66] sts. Working inc as set above, cont in st st, inc 1 st at each end of every foll 6th(6th,6th,4th,4th,4th) row to 92(100,106,112,118,128) sts. Cont straight in st st until sleeve meas 46(46,47,47,48,48)cm /18(18,18½,18½,19,19)in, ending with a WS row.

Place stitch markers at each end of last row to denote start of armholes.

Next row (RS): K2, Sl 1, K1, psso, K to last 4 sts, K2tog, K2. 90 [98,104,110,116,126] sts.

Next row (WS): Purl.

Next row: Knit.

Next row: Purl.

Rep last 4 rows twice more. 86[94,100,106,112,122] sts.

Next row (RS): K2, Sl 1, K1, psso, K to last 4 sts, K2tog, K2. 84 [92,98,104,110,120] sts

Next row (WS): P2, Sl 1 purlwise, P1, psso, P to last 4 sts, P2tog, P2. 82 [90,96,102,108,118] sts.

Rep last 2 rows to 16 sts.

Cast off.

MAKING UP

Press as described on the information page.

Join both shoulder seams using mattress stitch.

NECKBAND

With RS facing, using 4mm (US 6) circular needles, knit 81(86,91,97,103,109) sts from right front stitch holder, pick up and knit 3 sts down right back neck, knit 26(26,28,28,30,30) sts from back neck stitch holder, pick up and knit 3 sts up left back neck, knit 81(86,91,97,103,109) sts from left front stitch holder. 194 [204,216,228,242,254] sts.

Starting with a P row, work in st st for 8cm/3¼in, ending with a WS row.

Cast off.

Sew in sleeves.

Join side and sleeve seams.

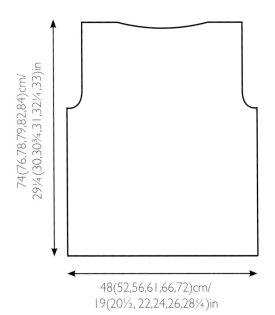

74(76,78,79,82,84)cm/
29¼(30,30¾,31,32¼,33)in

48(52,56,61,66,72)cm/
19(20½, 22,24,26,28¼)in

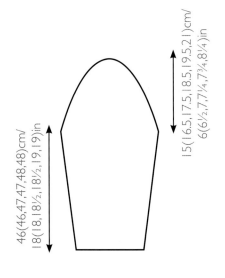

15(16.5,17.5,18.5,19.5,21)cm/
6(6½,7,7¼,7¾,8¼)in

46(46,47,47,48,48)cm/
18(18,18½,18½,19,19)in

Ella

SIZES

To fit bust

71-76	81-86	91-97	102-107	112-117	122-127	cm
28-30	32-34	36-38	40-42	44-46	48-50	in

Actual size

115	122	128	134	140	146	cm
45¼	48	50½	52¾	55	57	½in

YARN

Rowan Kid Classic

14	14	15	15	16	16	× 50g

(photographed in shade Drought 876)

NEEDLES

4.5mm (no 7) (US 7) needles

4.5mm (no 7) (US 7) circular needles at least 120cm/47in long

TENSION

26 stitches and 29 rows to 10cm/4in measured over K2, P2 rib using 4.5mm (US 7) needles

EXTRAS

Cable needle

Stitch holder

SPECIAL ABBREVIATIONS

C4F – slip next 2 sts onto cable needle and hold at front of work, K2, K2 sts from cable needle.

C4B – slip next 2 sts onto cable needle and hold at back of work, K2, K2 sts from cable needle.

2/2 RPC – slip next 2 sts onto cable needle and hold at back of work, K2, P2 sts from cable needle.

2/2 LPC – slip next 2 sts onto cable needle and hold at front of work, P2, K2 sts from cable needle.

CABLE PATTERN

Row 1 (WS): P2, K6, P4, K2, P2, K1, P2, K2, P4, K6, P2.

Row 2 (RS): K2, P6, C4F, P2, K2, P1, K2, P2, C4B, P6, K2.

Row 3 and all following WS rows:

Knit the knit stitches, purl the purl stitches.

Row 4: K2, P6, K4, C4B, P1, C4F, K4, P6, K2.

Row 6: K2, P6, K2, C4B, K2, P1, K2, C4F, K2, P6, K2.

Row 8: K2, P6, C4B, K4, P1, K4, C4F, P6, K2.

Row 10: K2, P4, C4B, K2, C4F, P1, C4B, K2, C4F, P4, K2.

Row 12: K2, P4, K4, 2/2 RPC, K2, P1, K2, 2/2 LPC, K4, P4, K2.

Row 14: K2, P4, K2, C4B, P2, K2, P1, K2, P2, C4F, K2, P4, K2.

Row 16: K2, P4, C4B, K2, P2, K2, P1, K2, P2, K2, C4F, P4, K2.

Row 18: As row 3.

Row 20: K2, P4, K2, 2/2 RPC, P2, K2, P1, K2, P2, 2/2 LPC, K2, P4, K2.

Row 22: K2, P4, C4B, P4, K2, P1, K2, P4, C4F, P4, K2.

Row 24: K2, P2, C4B, K2, P4, K2, P1, K2, P4, K2, C4F, P2, K2.

Row 26: K2, C4B, K4, P4, K2, P1, K2, P4, K4, C4F, K2.

Row 28: C4B, K2, 2/2 RPC, P4, K2, P1, K2, P4, 2/2 LPC, K2, C4F.

Row 30: K4, C4B, P6, K2, P1, K2, P6, C4F, K4.

Row 32: K2, C4B, K2, P6, K2, P1, K2, P6, K2, C4F, K2.

Row 34: 2/2 RPC, K4, P6, K2, P1, K2, P6, K4, 2/2 LPC.

Row 36: K2, P2, C4B, P6, K2, P1, K2, P6, C4F, P2, K2.

Row 38: K2, P2, C4B, P6, K2, P1, K2, P6, C4F, P2, K2.

Row 40: K2, C4F, K2, P6, K2, P1, K2, P6, K2, C4B, K2.

Row 42: K4, C4F, P6, K2, P1, K2, P6, C4B, K4.

Row 44: C4F, K2, C4F, P4, K2, P1, K2, P4, C4B, K2, C4B.

Row 46: K2, 2/2 LPC, K4, P4, K2, P1, K2, P4, K4, 2/2 RPC, K2.

Row 48: K2, P2, 2/2 LPC, K2, P4, K2, P1, K2, P4, K2, 2/2 RPC, P2, K2.

Row 50: K2, P4, C4F, P4, K2, P1, K2, P4, C4B, P4, K2.

Row 52: K2, P4, K2, C4F, P2, K2, P1, K2, P2, C4B, K2, P4, K2.
Row 54: K2, P4, K6, P2, K2, P1, K2, P2, K6, P4, K2.
Row 56: K2, P4, C4F, K2, P2, K2, P1, K2, P2, K2, C4B, P4, K2.
Row 58: K2, P4, K2, C4F, P2, K2, P1, K2, P2, C4B, K2, P4, K2.
Row 60: K2, P4, K4, C4F, K2, P1, K2, C4B, K4, P4, K2.
Row 62: K2, P4, 2/2 LPC, K2, C4F, P1, C4B, K2, 2/2 RPC, P4, K2.
Row 64: K2, P6, C4F, K4, P1, K4, C4B, P6, K2.
Row 66: K2, P6, K2, C4F, K2, P1, K2, C4B, K2, P6, K2.
Row 68: K2, P6, K4, 2/2 LPC, P1, 2/2 RPC, K4, P6, K2.

BACK

Using 4.5mm (US 7) needles, cast on 150(158,166,174,182,190) sts.
Next row (RS): *K2, P2, rep from * to last 2 sts, K2.
Next row (WS): P2,*K2, P2, rep from * to end.
Rep last 2 rows until back meas 8cm/3¼in, ending
with a RS row and dec 1 st at each end of last row.
148[156,164,172,180,188] sts.

Next row (WS): P1, K2, (P2, K2) 9(10,11,12,13,14) times,
work row 1 of cable pattern, P1, K2, P1, work row 1 of cable
pattern, (K2, P2) 9(10,11,12,13,14) times, K2, P1.
Next row (RS): K1, P2 (K2, P2) 9(10,11,12,13,14) times, work
row 2 of cable pattern, K1, P2, K1, work row 2 of cable pattern,
(P2, K2) 9 (10,11,12,13,14) times, P2, K1.
Working rows as set above, starting with row 3 of cable
pattern and working cable rows 1 - 68 throughout,
cont in patt until back meas 85(86,87,88,89,90)cm
/33½(33¾,34¼,34¾,35,35½)in, ending with a WS row.

Shape shoulders and back neck

Cont in patt, cast off 27(29,31,33,35,37) sts at beg of next
4 rows. 40 sts.
Slip rem 40 sts onto a stitch holder.

LEFT FRONT

Using 4.5mm (US 7) needles, cast on 86(90,94,98,98,102) sts.
Next row (RS): *K2, P2, rep from * to last 2 sts, K2.
Next row (WS): P2, *K2, P2, rep from * to end.
Rep last 2 rows until left front meas 8cm/3¼in, ending with
a RS row.

Next row (WS): P2, K2, work row 1 of cable pattern,
P1, (K2, P2) to end.

Next row (RS): (K2, P2) 12(13,14,15,15,16) times, K1,
work row 2 of cable pattern, P2, K2.
Working rows as set above, starting with row 3 of cable
pattern and working cable rows 1 - 68 throughout, cont
in patt until left front meas 39(40,41,42,49,50)cm
/15¼(15¾,16¼,16½,19¼,19¾)in, ending with a WS row.

Shape front slope

Keep cable pattern correct throughout.
Next row (RS): Patt to last 44 sts, patt2tog, patt to end.
85 [89,93,97,97,101] sts.
Work 3 rows in patt incorporating decreased st into pattern.
Rep last 4 rows to 54(58,62,66,70,74) sts.
Cont straight in patt until left front matches back to start of
shoulder shaping, ending with a WS row.

Cont in patt, cast off 27(29,31,33,35,37) sts at beg of next and
foll alt row. 0 sts.
Fasten off.

RIGHT FRONT

Using 4.5mm (US 7) needles, cast on 86(90,94,98,98,102) sts.
Next row (RS): *K2, P2, rep from * to last 2 sts, K2.
Next row (WS): P2, *K2, P2, rep from * to end.
Rep last 2 rows until right front meas 8cm/3¼in, ending with
a RS row.

Next row (WS): (P2, K2) 12(13,14,15,15,16) times,
P1, work row 1 of cable pattern, K2, P2.
Next row (RS): K2, P2, work row 2 of cable pattern,
K1, (P2, K2) to end.

Working rows as set above, starting with row 3 of cable
pattern and working cable rows 1 - 68 throughout,
cont in patt until right front meas 39(40,41,42,49,50)cm
/15¼(15¾,16¼,16½,19¼,19¾)in, ending with a RS row.

Shape front slope
Keep cable pattern correct throughout.
Next row (WS): Patt to last 44 sts, patt2tog, patt to end.
85 [89,93,97,97,101] sts.
Work 3 rows in patt incorporating decreased st into pattern.
Rep last 4 rows to 54(58,62,66,70,74) sts.

Cont straight in patt until right front matches back to start of shoulder shaping ending with a WS row.

Cont in patt, cast off 27(29,31,33,35,37) sts at beg of next and foll alt row.
Fasten off.

SLEEVES (make two)

Using 4.5mm (US 7) needles, cast on 66(66,66,74,74,74) sts.
Next row (RS): *K2, P2, rep from * to last 2 sts, K2.
Next row (WS): P2, *K2, P2, rep from * to end.
Rep last 2 rows until sleeve meas 16cm/6¼in, ending with a RS row.

Next row (WS): (P2, K2) 4(4,4,5,5,5) times, P2, K6, P4, K2, P2, K2tog, P2, K2, P4, K6, P2, (K2, P2) to end. 65[65,65,73,73,73] sts.

Next row (RS): (K2, P2) 4(4,4,5,5,5) times, work row 2 of cable pattern, (P2, K2) to end.
Working rows as set above, starting with row 3 of cable pattern and working cable rows 1 - 68 throughout, inc 1 st at each end of every following 4th row to 127(129,133,135,143,145) sts, incorporating increased sts into rib pattern.

Cont in patt until sleeve meas 45(46,46,47,48,49)cm /17¾(18,18,18½,19,19¼)in, ending with a WS row.
Cast off in patt.

MAKING UP

Press as described on the information page.
Join both shoulder seams using mattress stitch.

BAND

With RS facing, using 4.5mm (US 7) circular needles, pick up and knit 172(176,180,184,188,192) sts up right front, knit 40 sts from back neck stitch holder increasing 1 stitch at beg and end of these 40 sts, pick up and knit 172(176,180,184,188,192) sts down left front.
386 [394,402,410,418,426] sts.

Next row (WS): P2, *K2, P2, rep from * to end.
Next row (RS): *K2, P2, rep from * to last 2 sts, K2.
Rep last 2 rows until band meas 8cm/3¼in, ending with a WS row.
Cast off in rib.

Sew in sleeves.
Join side and sleeve seams, reversing sewing 8cm/3¼in along cuff for turn-back.

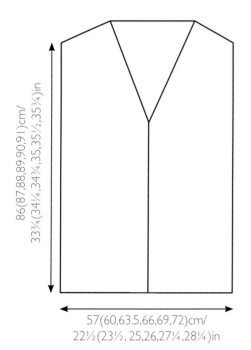

86(87,88,89,90,91)cm/
33¾(34¼,34¾,35,35½,35¾)in

57(60,63.5,66,69,72)cm/
22½(23½, 25,26,27¼,28¼)in

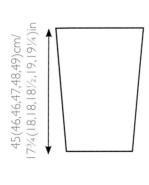

45(46,46,47,48,49)cm/
17¾(18,18,18½,19,19¼)in

Grace

SIZES

To fit bust

71-76	81-86	91-97	102-107	112-117	122-127	cm
28-30	32-34	36-38	40-42	44-46	48-50	in

Actual size

106	112	114.5	120	125.5	131	cm
41¾	44	45	47¼	49½	51½	in

YARN

Rowan Cocoon

10	10	11	11	12	13	× 100g

(photographed in shade Misty Rose 851)

NEEDLES

6mm (no 4) (US 10) needles

6mm (no 4) (US 10) circular needles at least 100cm/40in long

TENSION

14.5 stitches and 21 rows to 10cm/4in measured over stocking stitch using 6mm (US 10) needles.

EXTRAS

Stitch holders

BACK

Using 6mm (US 10) needles, cast on 77(81,83,87,91,95) sts. Starting with a K row, work in st st until back meas 68 (70,72,72,74,74)cm / 26¾(27½,28¼,28¼,29¼,29¼)in, ending with a WS row.

Shape armholes

Continue in st st, cast off 6 sts at beg of next 2 rows.
65 [69,71,75,79,83] sts.
Next row (RS): K2, Sl 1, K1, psso, K to last 4 sts, K2tog, K2.
63 [67,69,73,77,81] sts.
Next row (WS): P to end.

Cont straight in st st until armhole meas 21(21,22,22,23,23)cm /8¼ (8¼,8¾,8¾,9,9)in, ending with a WS row.

Shape shoulders and back neck

Continue in st st, cast off 9(10,10,11,12,13) sts at beg of next 4 rows.

Slip rem 27(27,29,29,29,29) sts onto a stitch holder.

LEFT FRONT

Using 6mm (US 10) needles, cast on 38(40,41,42,44,47) sts. Starting with a K row, work in st st until front meas 49(51,54,54,57,57)cm/19¼ (20,21¼,21¼,22½,22½)in, ending with a WS row.

Next row (RS): K to last 4 sts, K2tog, K2. 37[39,40,41,43,46] sts. Working dec as set above, cont in st st, dec 1 st at front slope edge of every following 6 th row to 31(33,34,35,37,40) sts **AND AT SAME TIME** when work meas 68(70,72,72,74,74)cm /26¾(27½,28¼,28¼,29¼,29¼)in, ending with a WS row:
Next row (RS): Cast off 6 sts and K to end.
25[27,28,29,31,34] sts.

Cont in st st until left front matches length of back. 18[20,20,22,24,26] sts.

Cast off 9(10,10,11,12,13) sts at beg of next and foll alt row. Fasten off.

RIGHT FRONT

Using 6mm (US 10) needles, cast on 38(40,41,42,44,47) sts.
Starting with a K row, work in st st until front meas
49(51,54,54,57,57)cm/19¼(20,21¼,21¼,22½,22½)in,
ending with a WS row.

Next row (RS): K2, K2tog, K to end. 37 [39,40,41,43,46] sts.
Working dec as set above, cont in st st, dec 1 st at front slope
edge of every following 6 th row to 31(33,34,35,37,40) sts
AND AT SAME TIME when work meas 68(70,72,72,74,74)cm
/26¾(27½,28¼,28¼,29¼,29¼)in, ending with a RS row.
Next row (WS): Cast off 6 sts and P to end.
25 [27,28,29,31,34] sts.
Cont in st st until right front matches length of back.
18 [20,20,22,24,26] sts.
Cast off 9(10,10,11,12,13) sts at beg of next and foll alt row.
Fasten off.

SLEEVES (make two)

Using 6mm (US 10) needles, cast on 34(34,34,38,38,38) sts.
Starting with a K row, work 2 rows in st st.

Next row (RS): K2, M1, K to last 2 sts, M1, K2.
36[36,36,40,40,40] sts.
Working inc as set above, cont in st st, and inc 1 st at each
end of every foll 6 th row to 60(60,64,64,66,66) sts.
Cont straight in st st until sleeve meas 43(43,44,44,45,45)cm
/17(17,17¼,17¼,17¾,17¾)in, ending with a WS row.

Shape armholes

Cont in st st, cast off 6 sts at beg of next 2 rows.
48[48,52,52,54,54] sts.
Next row (RS): K2, Sl 1, K1, psso, K to last 4 sts, K2tog,
K2. 46 [46,50,50,52,52] sts.
Next row (WS): Purl.
Rep last 2 rows to 20(20,22,22,24,24) sts, ending with a
WS row.
Next row (RS): K2, Sl 1, K1, psso, K to last 4 sts, K2tog,
K2. 18[18,20,20,22,22] sts.
Next row (WS): P2, Sl 1 purlwise, psso, P to last 4 sts,
P2tog, P2. 16[16,18,18,20,20] sts.
Rep last 2 rows to 10 sts, ending with a WS row.
Cast off.

MAKING UP

Press as described on the information page.
Join both shoulder seams using mattress stitch.

BAND

With RS facing, using 6mm (US 10) circular needles
and starting at right front cast-on edge, pick up and knit
86(90,94,94,102,102) sts evenly up right front to start of
slope shaping, pick up and knit 70 sts up right front slope, knit
27(27,29,29,29,29) sts from back neck stitch holder, pick up
and knit 70 sts down left front slope then pick up and knit
86(90,94,94,102,102) sts down left front.
339[347,357,357,373,373] sts.
Cast off knitwise.

POCKETS (make two)

Using 6mm (US 10) needles, cast on 22 sts.
Starting with a K row, work 30 rows in st st.
Cast off.

Sew in sleeves.
Join side and sleeve seams.
Using the photograph as a guide, attach pockets.

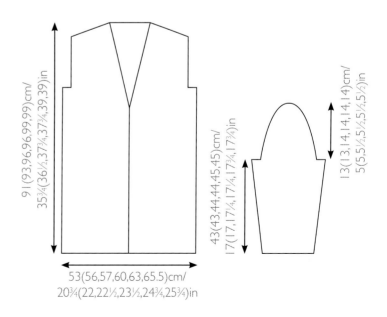

91(93,96,96,99,99)cm/
35¾(36½,37¾,37¾,39,39)in

43(43,44,44,45,45)cm/
17(17,17¼,17¼,17¾,17¾)in

53(56,57,60,63,65.5)cm/
20¾(22,22½,23½,24¾,25¾)in

13(13,14,14,14,14)cm/
5(5,5½,5½,5½,5½)in

Ida

SIZES

To fit bust

71-76	81-86	91-97	102-107	112-117	122-127	cm
28-30	32-34	36-38	40-42	44-46	48-50	in

Actual size

113	118	124	129	135	138	cm
44½	46½	48¾	50¾	53¼	54¼	in

YARN

Rowan Brushed Fleece

7	7	8	8	9	9	x 50g

(photographed in shade Cairn 263)

NEEDLES

7mm (no 2) (US 10.5) needles

TENSION

11 stitches and 16 rows to 10cm/4in measured over stocking stitch using 7mm (US 10.5) needles.

BACK AND FRONT (both alike)

Using 7mm (US 10.5) needles, cast on 62(65,68,71,74,76) sts.
Starting with a K row, work in st st until back meas 48(48.5,49,49,50,50)cm/19(19,19¼,19¼,19¾,19¾)in, ending with a WS row.

Shape armholes

Continue in st st, cast off 3 sts at beg of next 2 rows. 56[59,62,65,68,70] sts.
Next row (RS): K2, Sl 1, K1, psso, K to last 4 sts, K2tog, K2. 54[57,60,63,66,68] sts.
Next row (WS): Purl.
Rep last 2 rows to 50(53,56,59,62,64) sts.
Cont straight in st st until armhole meas 23(23.5,24,25,25,26)cm /9(9¼,9½,9¾,9¾,10¼)in, ending with a WS row.

Shape shoulders and neckband

Continue in st st, cast off 10(10,11,12,13,14) sts at beg of next 2 rows. 30[33,34,35,36,36] sts.

Next row (RS): K2, Sl 1, K1, psso, K to last 4 sts, K2tog, K2. 28[31,32,33,34,34] sts.
Continue in st st, working dec as set above, dec 1 st at each end of every foll 4th row to 24(25,26,27,28,28) sts.
Work 1 row.
Cast off.

SLEEVES (make two)

Using 7mm (US 10.5) needles, cast on 24(24,26,26,28,28) sts.
Starting with a K row, work 2 rows in st st.
Next row (RS): K2, M1, K to last 2 sts, M1, K2. 26[26,28,28,30,30] sts.
Cont in st st, working inc as set above, inc 1 st at each end of every foll 4th row to 50(52,52,54,56,58) sts.
Cont in st st until sleeve meas 43(43,44,44,45,45)cm /17(17,17¼,17¼,17¾,17¾)in, ending with a WS row.
Cont in st st, cast off 3 sts at beg of next 2 rows. 44[46,46,48,50,52] sts.
Next row (RS): K2, Sl 1, K1, psso, K to last 4 sts, K2tog, K2. 42[44,44,46,48,50] sts.
Next row (WS): Purl.
Rep last 2 rows twice more. 38[40,40,42,44,46] sts.
Cast off.

MAKING UP

Press as described on the information page.

Join both shoulder and neckband seams using
mattress stitch.

Sew in sleeves.

Join side and sleeve seams.

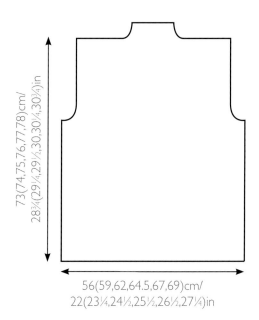

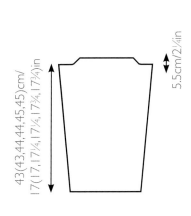

16 stitches and 20 rows to 10cm/4in measured over stocking stitch using 5mm (US 8) needles and 1 strand of Rowan Pure Wool Worsted and 1 strand of Rowan Kidsilk Haze held together.

EXTRAS
Stitch holders
Stitch markers

BACK
Using 4.5mm (US 7) needles and 1 strand of each yarn held together throughout, cast on 74(82,92,100,108,116) sts.
Next row (RS): *K1, P1, rep from * to end.
Next row (WS): *K1, P1, rep from * to end.
Rep last 2 rows until back meas 8cm/3¼ in, ending with a WS row and inc 1 st at end of last row. 75[83,93,101,109,117] sts.

Change to 5mm (US 8) needles.
Starting with a K row, work in st st until back meas 45(47,49,51,53,55)cm/17¾(18½,19¼,20,20¾,21¾)in, ending with a WS row.

Shape shoulders and back neck
Cont in st st, cast off 11(13,15,17,19,21) sts at beg of foll 4 rows. Leave rem 31(31,33,33,33,33) sts on a stitch holder.

Place stitch markers 20(20,21,22,22,23)cm /7¾(7¾,8¼,8¾,8¾,9)in down from start of shoulder shaping to denote start of armholes.

FRONT
Using 4.5mm (US 7) needles and 1 strand of each yarn held together throughout, cast on 74(82,92,100,108,116) sts.

Next row (RS): *K1, P1, rep from * to end.
Next row (WS): *K1, P1, rep from * to end.
Rep last 2 rows until front meas 8cm/3¼in, ending with a WS row and inc 1 st at end of last row. 75[83,93,101,109,117] sts.

Change to 5mm (US 8) needles.
Starting with a K row, work in st st until front meas 36(38,40,42,44,46)cm/14¼(15,15¾,16½,17¼,18)in, ending with a WS row.

Mable

SIZES
To fit bust

71-76	81-86	91-97	102-107	112-117	122-127	cm
28-30	32-34	36-38	40-42	44-46	48-50	in

Actual size

91	101	115	125	135	145	cm
35¾	39¾	45¼	49¼	53¼	57	in

YARN
Rowan Pure Wool Worsted & Rowan Kidsilk Haze

5	5	6	6	7	7	× 100g

(photographed in shade Navy 149)

5	5	6	6	7	7	× 25g

(photographed in shade Turkish Plum 660)

NEEDLES
4.5mm (no 7) (US 7) needles
5mm (no 6) (US 8) needles

Shape front neck

Next row (RS): K31(35,39,43,46,50), turn, and leave rem sts on a stitch holder.

Next row (WS): P2, Sl 1 purlwise, P1, psso, P to end. 30[34,38,42,45,49] sts.

Next row: K to last 4 sts, K2tog, K2. 29[33,37,41,44,48] sts.

Rep last 2 rows to 22(26,30,34,38,42) sts.

Cont straight in st st until front matches back to start of shoulder shaping, ending with WS row..

Shape shoulders

Cont in st st, cast off 11(13,15,17,19,21) sts at beg of next and foll alt row.

Slip centre 13(13,15,15,17,17) sts onto a second stitch holder.

With RS facing rejoin yarn and K to end.

Work as for other side, reversing shapings.

Place stitch markers 20(20,21,22,22,23)cm /7¾(7¾,8¼,8¾,8¾,9)in down from start of shoulder shaping to denote start of armholes.

SLEEVES (make two)

Using 4.5mm (US 7) needles and 1 strand of each yarn held together throughout, cast on 42(42,42,44,44,44) sts.

Next row (RS): *K1, P1, rep from * to end.

Next row (WS): *K1, P1, rep from * to end.

Rep last 2 rows until sleeve meas 8cm/3¼in, ending with a WS row.

Change to 5mm (US 8) needles.

Next row (RS): K2, M1, K to last 2 sts, M1, K2. 44[44,44,46,46,46] sts.

Working inc as set above, cont in st st, inc 1 st at each end of every foll 6th row to 64(64,68,70,70,74) sts.

Cont straight in st st until sleeve meas 43(44,45,46,47,48)cm /17(17¼,17¾,18,18½,19)in, ending with a WS row.

Cast off.

MAKING UP

Press as described on the information page.

Join right shoulder seam.

NECKBAND

With RS facing, using 4.5mm (US 7) needles and 1 strand of each yarn held together throughout, pick up and knit 24(24,28,28,28,28) sts down left front neck, knit 13(13,15,15,17,17) sts from front neck stitch holder, pick up and knit 24(24,28,28,28,28) sts up right front neck, knit 31(31,33,33,33,33) sts from back neck stitch holder. 92[92,104,104,106,106] sts.

Next row (WS): *K1, P1, rep from * to end.

Next row (RS): *K1, P1, rep from * to end.

Rep last 2 rows until neck meas 22cm/8¾in, ending with a WS row.

Cast off in patt.

Join left shoulder and neck seam.

Using stitch markers as a guide, sew in sleeves.

Sew side and sleeve seams.

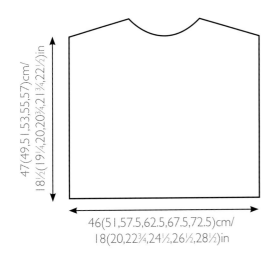

47(49,51,53,55,57)cm/ 18½(19¼,20,20¾,21¾,22½)in

46(51,57.5,62.5,67.5,72.5)cm/ 18(20,22¾,24½,26½,28½)in

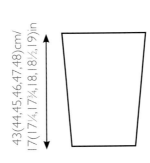

43(44,45,46,47,48)cm/ 17(17¼,17¾,18,18½,19)in

Marie

SIZES

To fit bust

| 71-76 | 81-86 | 91-97 | 102-107 | 112-117 | 122-127 | cm |
| 28-30 | 32-34 | 36-38 | 40-42 | 44-46 | 48-50 | in |

Actual size

| 101 | 103.5 | 108 | 112 | 128 | 138 | cm |
| 39¾ | 40¾ | 42½ | 44 | 50½ | 54¼ | in |

YARN

Rowan Kid Classic

| 10 | 10 | 11 | 11 | 12 | 12 | x 50g |

(photographed in shade Pumice 888)

NEEDLES

1 pair of 4mm (no 8) (US 6) needles

TENSION

28 stitches and 28 rows to 10cm/4in measured over K1, P1 rib using 4mm (US 6) needles.

EXTRAS

Stitch holder

Stitch markers

BACK

Using 4mm (US 6) needles, cast on 141(145,151,157,179,193) sts.

Next row (RS): *K1, P1, rep from * to last st, K1.

Next row (WS): P1, *K1, P1, rep from * to end.

Rep last 2 rows until back meas 39(41,42,43,44,45)cm /15¼(16¼,16½,17,17¼,17¾)in, ending with a WS row.

Shape sleeve extensions

Taking increases into pattern, cont in rib as set, inc 1 st at each end of every row to 219 [223,229,235,257,271] sts.

Place stitch markers at each end of last row to denote start of armhole.

Cont straight in rib as set until armhole meas 15cm/6in, ending with a WS row.

Shape shoulders and back neck

Cont in rib as set, cast off 8(8,8,8,10,10) sts at beg of next 16(16,16,18,18,18) rows, then 7(9,12,7,0,7) sts on foll 2 rows. 77 sts.

Cast off in rib.

FRONT

Using 4mm (US 6) needles, cast on 141(145,151,157,179,193) sts.

Next row (RS): *K1, P1, rep from * to last st, K1.

Next row (WS): P1, *K1, P1, rep from * to end.

Rep last 2 rows until front meas 39(41,42,43,44,45)cm /15¼(16¼,16½,17,17¼,17¾)in, ending with a WS row.

Shape sleeve extensions and front neck

Taking increases into pattern, cont in rib as set, inc 1 st at each end of next 28 rows. 197[201,207,213,235,249] sts.

Next Row (RS): Inc 1 st at beg of next row, work across row in patt until you have 99(101,104,107,118,125) sts on right hand needle.

Leave rem 99(101,104,107,118,125) sts on a stitch holder.

Left front

Next row (WS): Patt 3 sts, patt2tog, patt to end, inc 1 st at end of row. 99 [101,104,107,118,125] sts.

Next row (RS): Inc 1 st, patt to end.

100 [102,105,108,119,126] sts.

Rep last 2 rows four more times. 104[106,109,112,123,130] sts.

Place stitch marker at end of last row to denote start of armhole.

Cont in pattern, dec 1 st on every foll WS row to 94(96,99,102,113,120) sts.

Then dec 1 st at neck edge on every foll row to 71[73,76,79,90,97] sts.

Cont straight in rib until work meas 15cm/6in from stitch marker.

Shape shoulders

Cast off 8(8,8,8,10,10) sts at beg of next 8(8,8,9,9,9) alt rows. 7 [9,12,7,0,7] sts.

Work 2 rows in rib.

Cast off in rib.

Right front

With RS facing rejoin yarn to 99(101,104,107,118,125) sts on stitch holder, casting off first stitch and inc 1 st at end of row. 99[101,104,107,118,125] sts.

Work as for left front, reversing shapings.

SLEEVES (make two)

Using 4mm (US 6) needles, cast on 57(57,61,61,65,65) sts.

Next row (RS): *K1, P1, rep from * to last st, K1.

Next row (WS): P1, *K1, P1, rep from * to end.

Taking inc into pattern, cont in rib as set inc 1 st at each end of next and every foll alt row to 83 sts.

Cont in rib until sleeve meas 33(34,35,36,37,38)cm /13(13½,13¾,14¼,14½,15)in, ending with a WS row.

Cast off in rib.

MAKING UP

Press as described on the information page.

Join both shoulder seams using mattress stitch.

Sew in sleeves.

Join side seams starting 10cm/4in up from cast-on edge.

Join sleeve extensions and sleeve seams.

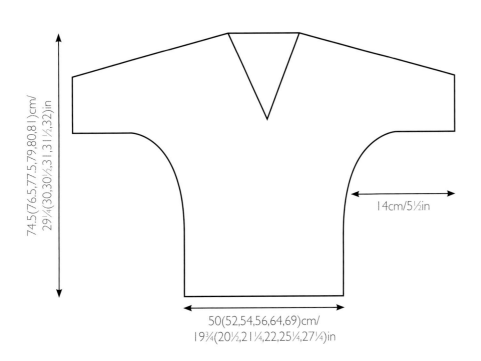

74.5(76.5,77.5,79,80,81)cm/
29¼(30,30½,31,31½,32)in

14cm/5½in

50(52,54,56,64,69)cm/
19¾(20½,21¼,22,25¼,27¼)in

Information

Sizing guide

To help you enjoy a great knitting experience and a well fitting garment please refer to our sizing guide which conforms to standard clothing sizes. Dimensions in our sizing guide are body measurements, not garment dimensions, please refer to the size diagram for this measurment.

SIZING GUIDE

UK SIZE	XS	S	M	L	XL	XXL	
DUAL SIZE	4/6	8/10	12/14	16/18	20/22	24/26	
To fit bust	28 – 30	32 – 34	36 – 38	40 – 42	44 – 46	48 – 50	inches
	71 – 76	81 – 86	91 - 97	102 – 107	112 – 117	122 – 127	cm
To fit waist	20 – 22	24 – 26	28 – 30	32 – 34	36 – 38	40 – 42	inches
	51 – 56	61 – 66	71 – 76	81 – 86	91 – 97	102 – 107	cm
To fit hips	30 – 32	34 – 36	38 – 40	42 – 44	46 – 48	50 – 52	inches

SIZING & SIZE DIAGRAM NOTE

The instructions are given for the smallest size. Where they vary, work the figures in brackets for the larger sizes. One set of figures refers to all sizes. Included with most patterns in this magazine is a 'size diagram' - see image on the right, of the finished garment and its dimensions. The measurement shown at the bottom of each 'size diagram' shows the garment width 2.5cm below the armhole shaping. To help you choose the size of garment to knit please refer to the sizing guide. Generally in the majority of designs the welt width (at the cast on edge of the garment) is the same width as the chest. However, some designs are 'A-Line' in shape or flared edge and in these cases welt width will be wider than the chest width.

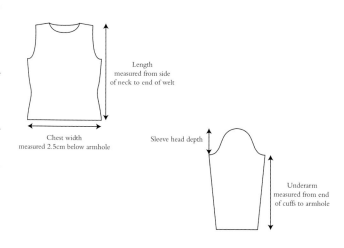

MEASURING GUIDE

For maximum comfort and to ensure the correct fit when choosing a size to knit, please follow the tips below when checking your size. Measure yourself close to your body, over your underwear and don't pull the tape measure too tight!

Bust/chest – measure around the fullest part of the bust/chest and across the shoulder blades.

Waist – measure around the natural waistline, just above the hip bone.

Hips – measure around the fullest part of the bottom.

If you don't wish to measure yourself, note the size of a favourite jumper that you like the fit of. Our sizes are now comparable to the clothing sizes from the major high street retailers, so if your favourite jumper is a size Medium or size 12, then our Medium should be approximately the same fit.

To be extra sure, measure your favourite jumper and then compare these measurements with the Rowan size diagram given at the end of the individual instructions.

Finally, once you have decided which size is best for you, please ensure that you achieve the tension required for the design you wish to knit.

Remember if your tension is too loose, your garment will be bigger than the pattern size and you may use more yarn. If your tension is too tight, your garment could be smaller than the pattern size and you will have yarn left over.

Furthermore if your tension is incorrect, the handle of your fabric will be too stiff or floppy and will not fit properly. It really does make sense to check your tension before starting every project.

Information

TENSION

Obtaining the correct tension is perhaps the single factor which can make the difference between a successful garment and a disastrous one. It controls both the shape and size of an article, so any variation, however slight, can distort the finished garment. Different designers feature in our books and it is their tension, given at the start of each pattern, which you must match. We recommend that you knit a square in pattern and/or stocking stitch (depending on the pattern instructions) of perhaps 5 - 10 more stitches and 5 - 10 more rows than those given in the tension note. Mark out the central 10cm square with pins. If you have too many stitches to 10cm try again using thicker needles, if you have too few stitches to 10cm try again using finer needles. Once you have achieved the correct tension your garment will be knitted to the measurements indicated in the
size diagram shown at the end of the pattern.

FINISHING INSTRUCTIONS

After working for hours knitting a garment, it seems a great pity that many garments are spoiled because such little care is taken in the pressing and finishing process. Follow the text below for a truly professional-looking garment.

PRESSING

Block out each piece of knitting and following the instructions on the ball band press the garment pieces, omitting the ribs. Tip: Take special care to press the edges, as this will make sewing up both easier and neater. If the ball band indicates that the fabric is not to be pressed, then covering the blocked out fabric with a damp white cotton cloth and leaving it to stand will have the desired effect. Darn in all ends neatly along the selvage edge or a colour join, as appropriate.

STITCHING

When stitching the pieces together, remember to match areas of colour and texture very carefully where they meet. Use a seam stitch such as back stitch or mattress stitch for all main knitting seams and join all ribs and neckband with mattress stitch, unless otherwise stated.

CONSTRUCTION

Having completed the pattern instructions, join left shoulder and neckband seams as detailed above. Sew the top of the sleeve to the body of the garment using the method detailed in the pattern, referring to the appropriate guide:

Straight cast-off sleeves: Place centre of cast-off edge of sleeve to shoulder seam. Sew top of sleeve to body, using markers as guidelines where applicable.

Square set-in sleeves: Place centre of cast-off edge of sleeve to shoulder seam. Set sleeve head into armhole, the straight sides at top of sleeve to form a neat right-angle to cast-off sts at armhole on back and front.

Shallow set-in sleeves: Place centre of cast off edge of sleeve to shoulder seam. Match decreases at beg of armhole shaping to decreases at top of sleeve. Sew sleeve head into armhole, easing in shapings.

Set-in sleeves: Place centre of cast-off edge of sleeve to shoulder seam. Set in sleeve, easing sleeve head into armhole.

Join side and sleeve seams.
Slip stitch pocket edgings and linings into place.
Sew on buttons to correspond with buttonholes.
Ribbed welts and neckbands and any areas of garter stitch should not be pressed.

PHOTOGRAPHY MODEL INFORMATION

The model in the photography wears a UK dress size 10 and is 5' 8" tall.

The photography garments were knitted in the following sizes;
Alice – One Size
Annie – Small
Betty – Small
Ella – Small
Grace – Extra Small
Ida – Small
Marie – Small
Mabel – Small

Information

ABBREVIATIONS

alt	alternate
beg	begin(ning)
cm	centimetres
cont	continue
dec	decrease(s)(ing)
DK	double knitting
foll(s)	follow(s)(ing)
g	grams
g st	garter stitch
in	inch(es)
inc	increase(s)(ing)
K	knit
Kfb	knit in front and back of stitch (makes 1 stitch)
M1	make 1 stitch by picking up loop betwee last and next stitch and working into the back of this loop
meas	measures
mm	millimetres
P	purl
patt	pattern
psso	pass slipped stitch over
rem	remain(ing)
rep	repeat
RS	right side of work
Sl 1	slip 1 stitch
st st	stocking stitch
st(s)	stitch(es)
tog	together
WS	wrong side of work

WASHCARE SYMBOLS

machine wash

hand wash

dry clean

iron

do not bleach

drying

Stockists

AUSTRALIA: Australian Country Spinners, Pty Ltd, Level 7, 409 St. Kilda Road, Melbourne Vic 3004.
Tel: 03 9380 3888   Fax: 03 9820 0989   Email: customerservice@auspinners.com.au

AUSTRIA: MEZ Harlander GmbH, Schulhof 6, 1. Stock, 1010 Wien, Austria
Tel: + 00800 26 27 28 00   Fax: (00) 49 7644 802-133
Email: verkauf.harlander@mezcrafts.com

BELGIUM: MEZ crafts Belgium NV, c/o MEZ GmbH, Kaiserstr.1, 79341 Kenzingen Germany
Tel: 0032 (0) 800 77 89 2   Fax: 00 49 7644 802 133   Email: sales.be-nl@mezcrafts.com

BULGARIA: MEZ Crafts Bulgaria EOOD, 7 Magnaurska Shkola Str., BG-1784 Sofia, Bulgaria
Tel: (+359 2) 976 77 41   Fax: (+359 2) 976 77 20   Email: office.bg@mezcrafts.com

CANADA: Sirdar USA Inc. 406 20th Street SE, Hickory, North Carolina, USA 28602
Tel: 828 404 3705   Fax: 828 404 3707   Email: sirdarusa@sirdar.co.uk

CHINA: Commercial agent Mr Victor Li, c/o MEZ GmbH Germany, Kaiserstr. 1, 79341 Kenzingen / Germany
Tel: (86- 21) 13816681825   Email: victor.li@mezcrafts.com

CHINA: SHANGHAI YUJUN CO.,LTD., Room 701 Wangjiao Plaza, No.175 Yan'an (E), 200002 Shanghai, China
Tel: +86 2163739785   Email: jessechang@vip.163.com

CYPRUS: MEZ Crafts Bulgaria EOOD, 7 Magnaurska Shkola Str., BG-1784 Sofia, Bulgaria
Tel: (+359 2) 976 77 41   Fax: (+359 2) 976 77 20
Email: marketing.cy@mezcrafts.com

CZECH REPUBLIC: Coats Czecho s.r.o.Staré Mesto 246 569 32
Tel: (420) 461616633   Email: galanterie@coats.com

DENMARK: Carl J. Permin A/S Egegaardsvej 28 DK-2610 Rødovre
Tel: (45) 36 72 12 00   Email: permin@permin.dk

ESTONIA: MEZ Crafts Estonia OÜ, Ampri tee 9/4, 74001 Viimsi Harjumaa
Tel: +372 630 6252   Email: info.ee@mezcrafts.com

FINLAND: Prym Consumer Finland Oy, Huhtimontie 6, 04200 KERAVA
Tel: +358 9 274871

FRANCE: 3bcom, 35 avenue de Larrieu, 31094 Toulouse cedex 01, France
Tel: 0033 (0) 562 202 096   Email: Commercial@3b-com.com

GERMANY: MEZ GmbH, Kaiserstr. 1, 79341 Kenzingen, Germany
Tel: 0049 7644 802 222   Email: kenzingen.vertrieb@mezcrafts.com
Fax: 0049 7644 802 300

GREECE: MEZ Crafts Bulgaria EOOD, 7 Magnaurska Shkola Str., BG-1784 Sofia, Bulgaria
Tel: (+359 2) 976 77 41   Fax: (+359 2) 976 77 20
Email: marketing.gr@mezcrafts.com

HOLLAND: G. Brouwer & Zn B.V., Oudhuijzerweg 69, 3648 AB Wilnis, Netherlands
Tel: 0031 (0) 297-281 557   Email: info@gbrouwer.nl

HONG KONG: East Unity Company Ltd, Unit B2, 7/F., Block B, Kailey Industrial Centre, 12 Fung Yip Street, Chai Wan
Tel: (852)2869 7110   Email: eastunityco@yahoo.com.hk

ICELAND: Carl J. Permin A/S Egegaardsvej 28 DK-2610 Rødovre
Tel: (45) 36 72 12 00   Email: permin@permin.dk

ITALY: Mez Cucirini Italy Srl, Viale Sarca, 223, 20126 MILANO
Tel: 0039 0264109080 Email: servizio.clienti@mezcrafts.com Fax: 02 64109080

JAPAN: Hobbyra Hobbyre Corporation, 23-37, 5-Chome, Higashi-Ohi, Shinagawa-Ku, 1400011 Tokyo.   Tel: +81334721104
Daidoh International, 3-8-11 Kudanminami Chiyodaku, Hiei Kudan Bldg 5F, 1018619 Tokyo.   Tel +81-3-3222-7076, Fax +81-3-3222-7066

KOREA: My Knit Studio, 3F, 144 Gwanhun-Dong, 110-300 Jongno-Gu, Seoul
Tel: 82-2-722-0006   Email: myknit@myknit.com

LATVIA: Coats Latvija SIA, Mukusalas str. 41 b, Riga LV-1004
Tel: +371 67 625173   Fax: +371 67 892758   Email: info.latvia@coats.com

LEBANON: y.knot, Saifi Village, Mkhalissiya Street 162, Beirut
Tel: (961) 1 992211   Fax: (961) 1 315553   Email: y.knot@cyberia.net.lb

LITHUANIA: MEZ Crafts Lithuania UAB, A. Juozapaviciaus str. 6/2, LT-09310 Vilnius
Tel: +370 527 30971   Fax: +370 527 2305   Email: info.lt@mezcrafts.com

LUXEMBOURG: Coats N.V., c/o Coats GmbH, Kaiserstr.1, 79341 Kenzingen, Germany
Tel: 00 49 7644 802 222   Fax: 00 49 7644 802 133
Email: sales.coatsninove@coats.com

MEXICO: Estambres Crochet SA de CV, Aaron Saenz 1891-7Pte, 64650 MONTERREY
TEL +52 (81) 8335-3870   Email: abremer@redmundial.com.mx

NEW ZEALAND: ACS New Zealand, P.O Box 76199, Northwood, Christchurch, New Zealand
Tel: 64 3 323 6665   Fax: 64 3 323 6660   Email: lynn@impactmg.co.nz

NORWAY: Carl J. Permin A/S Egegaardsvej 28 DK-2610 Rødovre
Tel: (45) 36 72 12 00   E-mail: permin@permin.dk

PORTUGAL: Mez Crafts Portugal, Lda – Av. Vasco da Gama, 774 - 4431-059 V.N, Gaia, Portugal Tel: 00 351 223 770700   Email: sales.iberia@mezcrafts.com

RUSSIA: Family Hobby, 124683, Moskau, Zelenograd, Haus 1505, Raum III
Tel.: 007 (499) 270-32-47 Handtel. 007 916 213 74 04 Email: tv@fhobby.ru
Web: www.family-hobby.ru

SINGAPORE: Golden Dragon Store, BLK 203 Henderson Rd #07-02, 159546 Henderson Indurstrial Park Singapore
Tel: (65) 62753517   Fax: (65) 62767112   Email: gdscraft@hotmail.com

SLOVAKIA: MEZ Crafts Slovakia, s.r.o. Seberíniho 1, 821 03 Bratislava, Slovakia
Tel: +421 2 32 30 31 19   Email: galanteria@mezcrafts.com

SOUTH AFRICA: Arthur Bales LTD, 62 4th Avenue, Linden 2195
Tel: (27) 11 888 2401 Fax: (27) 11 782 6137   Email: arthurb@new.co.za

SPAIN: MEZ Fabra Spain S.A, Avda Meridiana 350, pta 13 D, 08027 Barcelona
Tel: +34 932908400   Fax: +34 932908409   Email: atencion.clientes@mezcrafts.com

SWEDEN: Carl J. Permin A/S Egegaardsvej 28 DK-2610 Rødovre
Tel: (45) 36 72 12 00   E-mail: permin@permin.dk

SWITZERLAND: MEZ Crafts Switzerland GmbH, Stroppelstrasse20, 5417 Untersiggenthal, Switzerland
Tel: +41 00800 2627 2800   Fax: 0049 7644 802 133
Email: verkauf.ch@mezcrafts.com

TURKEY: MEZ Crafts Tekstil A.S, Kavacık Mahallesi, Ekinciler Cad. Necip Fazıl Sok. No.8 Kat: 5, 34810 Beykoz / Istanbul
Tel: +90 216 425 88 10

TAIWAN: Cactus Quality Co Ltd, 7FL-2, No. 140, Sec.2 Roosevelt Rd, Taipei, 10084 Taiwan, R.O.C.
Tel: 00886-2-23656527   Fax: 886-2-23656503   Email: cqcl@ms17.hinet.net

THAILAND: Global Wide Trading, 10 Lad Prao Soi 88, Bangkok 10310
Tel: 00 662 933 9019   Fax: 00 662 933 9110   Email: global.wide@yahoo.com

U.S.A.: Sirdar USA Inc. 406 20th Street SE, Hickory, North Carolina, USA 28602
Tel: 828 404 3705   Fax: 828 404 3707   Email: sirdarusa@sirdar.co.uk

U.K: Mez Crafts U.K, 17F Brooke's Mill, Armitage Bridge, Huddersfield, HD4 7NR
Web: www.mezcrafts.com   Tel: 01484 950630

For a more stockists in all countries please logon to www.knitrowan.com

With thanks

Quail Studio would like to thank our superb team of knitters, who work all hours to turn projects around. A big thanks to Jarek and his team for making the photography look fantastic, Our wonderful model Carol-Ann Dunbar for making the garments look amazing, and finally Amelia for technically checking the patterns.

We would also like to thank everyone who buys and knits from our publications. We are constantly evolving our design studio to ensure we are bringing current fashion trends and wearable designs to the hand knitting industry. Hearing all of your feedback and reactions to our collections is what drives and shapes Quail Studio. We thank you for joining us on our journey.

Finally, we must thank all of the team at Rowan for supporting our publications, and working with us to create designs we are proud of, in a vast array of beautiful yarns.